the rules

A Man's
Guide to Life

Esquire

the rules

A Man's
Guide to Life

HEARST BOOKS

A division of Sterling Publishing Co., Inc.

New York / London

www.sterlingpublishing.com

The Library of Congress has cataloged the first edition
as follows:
Esquire : the rules : a man's guide to life / the editors
of Esquire magazine ; foreword, David Granger.
  p. cm.
Includes index.
  ISBN 1-58816-244-3
1. Conduct of life—Humor. 2. American wit and
humor. I. Esquire, inc.
  PN6231.C6142 E68 2003
  818' .60208—dc21
                                    2002151187

10 9 8 7 6 5 4

Published by Hearst Books,
A Division of Sterling Publishing Co., Inc.
387 Park Avenue South, New York, N.Y. 10016

Esquire and Hearst Books are trademarks
of Hearst Communications, Inc.

www.esquire.com

Produced by Blue Steel Communications,
Brooklyn, NY
Design: Frank Marchese

Distributed in Canada by Sterling Publishing
c/o Canadian Manda Group, 165 Dufferin Street
Toronto, Ontario, Canada M6K 3H6

Distributed in Australia by Capricorn Link (Australia)
Pty. Ltd.
P.O. Box 704, Windsor, NSW 2756 Australia

For information about custom editions, special sales,
premium and corporate purchases, please contact
Sterling Special Sales Department at 800-805-5489
or specialsales@sterlingpub.com.

Manufactured in China

Sterling ISBN-13: 978-1-58816-466-7
ISBN-10: 1-58816-466-7

acknowledgments

Esquire's Rules-makers include:

Ted Allen
Tim Carvell
Matt Claus
Brian Frazer
David Granger
Lauren Iannotti
A.J. Jacobs
David Jacobson
David Katz
Scott Omelianuk
Evan Rothman
Mike Sachs
Andy Ward

foreword

Seven years ago, up in *Esquire's* research library, behind the Periodicals Index and stacks of old issues of *Popular Mechanics*, we discovered a leather-bound, hand-calligraphed tome. Engraved in the leather cover were two simple words: The Rules.

Since that day, on the third Tuesday of every month, a staff member has made his pilgrimage to the Book. He opens it, jots down whichever maxims catch his eye and scurries back to his cubicle. We then, month after month, offer our findings to our faithful readers.

At first glance, some of them appear to be more opinion (Rule No. 176: The best instrument is the cello.). Some appear to be the products of moments of exasperation with the world (Rule No. 96: The dumber the man, the louder he talks.). Others the product of moments of enthusiasm or hysteria (Rule No. 193: It's always time for pie!). But, no, these are rules. They have stood the test of time and they have been bound between the covers of a BOOK. They are, therefore, true.

What we at *Esquire*, the magazine, try to do month after month is mix the lessons the world hurls at us on a daily basis with a sense of the absurd. The Rules contained herein may not be a guide to every single facet of a man's life, but they provide a way—through either advice or humor—to get through most of it, one rule at a time.

What we offer here is an expanded version of our original Rules Book. It is just a fraction of the plentitude of wisdom contained in the rules. More will leach out, in the magazine and in future volumes, one third Tuesday of each month at a time.

Courage,
David Granger
Editor in Chief

Rule No. **1**:

When aliens **talk,**
they never use
contractions.

Rule No. **2**:

Old people
always have
exact change.

MEN

Rule No. **3**:

Do not **trust** a man
who calls the
bathroom
"the **little**
boys' room."

Rule No. 4:

When someone says he is "pumped" about something, it usually means he's about to do something stupid.

Rule No. 5:

Women who sound sexy on the radio weigh 377 pounds.

Rule No. 6:

For every Tom Hanks, there's a Peter Scolari.

Rule No. 7:

Wow is not a verb.

Rule No. 8:

Sitcom characters watching porn always tilt their heads.

Rule No. 9:

In movies Italians can play Jews, and Jews can play Italians, but neither Jews nor Italians can play Lutherans.

Rule No. **10**:

Actors are short.
Comedians are shorter.

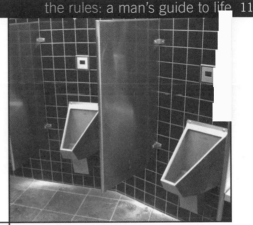

Rule No. **11**:

There is **nothing** that can be marketed that cannot be **better marketed** using the voice of James Earl Jones.

Rule No. **12**:

No talking at the urinal.

Rule No. **13**:

The team mascot
sleeps alone.

Rule No. **14**:

White cars
look good
only on Fantasy
Island.

Rule No. **15**:

Though jazz and
brunch
are acceptable
when separated,
the two should
never be
combined.

Rule No. 16:

People who **shell out** for HBO are not, in fact, under any obligation to **videotape** **programs** for people who **do not** shell out for **HBO**.

Rule No. 17:

The same **does** **not apply** to Showtime.

Rule No. **18**:

If you become annoyed with a telephone customer-service representative, be aware that the words "I'd like to speak to your supervisor" are generally understood to mean "I'd like to speak to your friend in the next cubicle, who will pretend to be your supervisor." Just so you know.

Rule No. **19**:

Unless you're a professional cyclist, or have lost a bet, take off the tight black Lycra biking shorts. Then burn them.

Rule No. **20**:

If Bill Gates were
good-looking
or **well dressed**,
people would
like him better.

Rule No. **21**:

Talk **half**
as much
as
you listen.

Rule No. **22**:

If you have been
drinking,
arrested,
or **touring** a
hostile land
full of gun-toting
fundamentalists,
or if you are the
lead singer
of Sugar Ray,
talk **one-fifth**
as much
as you listen.

Rule No. **23**:

Anyone who does anything on the advice of Joel Siegel deserves exactly what he gets.

Rule No. **24**:

A man in a minivan is half a man.

Rule No. **25**:

A man on a 1949 Indian motorcycle traveling at 93 miles an hour is 3.729 men, until he's cloven in twain by a bridge abutment, at which point he becomes two halves of a man.

Rule No. 27:

There is no **shame** in a good **mango.**

Rule No. 26:

Lesbians make the **best breakfasts.**

Rule No. 28:

If you are a mentally **retarded character** in a movie, it is imperative that your **pants** be **too short.**

Rule No. 29:

The only good white, dreadlocked street musician playing an extended version of "Tears in Heaven" is a dead white, dreadlocked street musician playing an extended version of "Tears in Heaven."

Rule No. 30:

There is no shame in the peanut butter sandwich.

Rule No. **31**:

The best **force** is centrifugal.

Rule No. **33**:

When it comes to luggage, **men don't pull.**

Rule No. **32**:

No matter how hard you **practice**, you cannot say the phrase, **"Yeah, right"** without sounding **sarcastic**.

Rule No. **34**:

People will compliment you on the **cheap artwork** you purchased at **IKEA**, but it will **feel hollow**.

Rule No. **35**:

Never **cook** with wine **bought** at a grocery store and labeled "**cooking** wine."

Rule No. **36**:

Never **cook** with wine that you **wouldn't** want to **drink**.

Rule No. **37**:

If you drink only Chateau Latour, **never cook**.

Rule No. 38:

There comes a time in any man's life when airborne livestock is no longer funny.

Rule No. 39:

A sandwich tastes exactly one-third better when it's made by someone else.

Rule No. 40:

For the last time, no goddamn Speedos.

Rule No. 41:

No man's **blender** is getting **enough** use these days.

Rule No. 42:

There is **no** dignified **way** to ask why you weren't **invited** to the pool **party**.

Rule No. 43:

It is **unnecessary** to compound the effect of **white shoes** by wearing a **white belt**.

Rule No. 44:

Never trust a man with pictures of **balloons** on his cheeks.

Rule No. 45:

The **soft taco** is the **only** **taco** that matters.

Rule No. 46:

When introducing yourself, you **will** **not amuse** anyone by adding, "And **I'm** an **alcoholic**."

Rule No. **47**:

Orange things
have to be
round.

Rule No. **48**:

The slang used
by teens in
TV dramas is
exactly 3.5 years
behind actual
slang.

Rule No. **49**:

Offering to rub oil
over the semi-naked
body of a total
stranger is no more
appropriate on the
beach than at a
bar mitzvah.

Rule No. 50:

No one looks cool playing the paddle game.

Rule No. 51:

Never trust anyone who, within five minutes of meeting you, tells you where he went to college.

Rule No. 52:

Especially if he refers to his college as "a little school in Boston" followed by a pause as he waits for you to ask its name.

Rule No. 54:

Never trust a man with two first names.

Rule No. 53:

The study of inert gases is best left to professionals.

Rule No. 55:

It then follows that you should steer well clear of Philip Michael Thomas.

Rule No. 56:

No mammals on the sweaters. Or belts.

Rule No. 57:

People with state pride are to be strictly avoided.

Rule No. 58:

No squatting in public.

Rule No. **59**:

Women named after a **month** of the year are usually **frisky**.

APRIL			
NESDAY	**THURSDAY**	**FRIDAY**	**SATURD**
3	☽ 4	5	
10	11	● 12	

Rule No. **60**:

From **least** chaotic to **most** chaotic: willy-**nilly**, hugger-**mugger**, hurly-**burly**, pell-**mell**.

Rule No. **61**:

Two-percent milk is bullshit.

Rule No. **63**:

Never trust an act of civil disobedience led by a disc jockey.

Rule No. **62**:

No matter how greasy the pizza is, you can't blot it with a paper towel and expect to be taken seriously.

Rule No. **64**:

People who tell you they love the taste of eggplant are lying.

Rule No. **65**:

Unless you are a **member** of the extended **Windsor family**, your summer **house** should **not** have a **name** like Emmerdale or Turkey Hill.

Rule No. **66**:

The **sniffing** of one's **finger** is a pleasure best indulged **discreetly**.

Rule No. **67**:

Inviting **others** to **sniff** one's finger: **more discreetly** still.

Rule No. **68**:

The ampersand should be more popular.

Rule No. **69**:

No group of people has worse hairstyles than men in government.

Rule No. **70**:

It's possible to actually become dumber by watching TV news-magazines.

Rule No. 71:

The only thing worse than words ending in "ly" are words ending in "ize."

Rule No. 72:

A man whose belt is fastened on the last hole is a desperate and resourceless-looking man.

Rule No. 73:

When describing the food served at a restaurant, the waiter should not use the phrase "I have a."

Rule No. 74:

Drugstores have the slowest cashiers.

Rule No. 75:

The two most terrifying words in the English language: humorous essay.

Rule No. 76:

There is nothing more fun than watching young couples in movies visit instant-photo booths.

Rule No. 77:

Never trust a man named after a body part.

Rule No. 78:

Especially if that body part is a pinkie.

Rule No. 79:

There is no shame in club soda and cranberry juice.

Rule No. **80**:

Come to think of it, the **Clapper** still **isn't** cool.

Rule No. **81**:

The **assassin's** compact, high-powered **rifle** is **packaged** in a briefcase by **Zero** Halliburton.

Rule No. **82**:

More **Calvin,** **less** Hobbes.

Rule No. **83**:

Stewardesses from **Third World** **airlines** are much more **attractive** than those from **developed** **nations.**

Rule No. 84:

Only the very rich can use summer and winter as verbs.

Rule No. 85:

Not even the Sultan of Brunei can use autumn as a verb.

Rule No. 86:

The best vocal register is basso profundo.

Rule No. 87:

Central and Middle America have similar names, but, in reality, they are very different.

Rule No. **88**:

People who live **inland** are **fatter** than those who live in **coastal** areas.

Rule No. **90**:

Never trust a man who uses **nautical metaphors**.

Rule No. **89**:

The *Wall Street Journal* is the proper **newspaper** for the **steam** room.

Rule No. **91**:

Never **play cards** with a man who wears a **visor**.

Rule No. **92**:

Barley is the most **underrated** grain.

Rule No. **93**:

Lips that have actually been **stung** by **bees** are **not** all that **erotic**.

Rule No. 95:

Right fielders
are the
ugliest.

Rule No. 94:

Shortstops are
the best-looking
baseball players,
followed by
first basemen
and pitchers,
in that order.

Rule No. 96:

The dumber
the man,
the louder he
talks.

Rule No. 97:

Never trust a man who claps backs.

Rule No. 98:

When it comes to author photos, hands should be at least eight inches from the face.

Rule No. 99:

If you must use a euphemism for masturbation, the only appropriate one is "scalping General Custer."

Rule No. **100**:

Born-again Christians have the most meticulously parted hair.

Rule No. **102**:

As a man gets older, his glasses and ears get larger at exactly the same rate.

Rule No. **101**:

It's borderline acceptable to spell A.M. as ayem It's absolutely unacceptable to spell P.M. as peeyem.

Rule No. **103**:

When a man turns 23, it's very important he stop using the word "party" as a verb.

Rule No. **104**:

The **road** to **hell** is **not** paved with good **intentions**. The road to hell is paved with **light-jazz** CDs, **herbal** teas, John **Tesh** specials, and **low-fat** cheese.

Rule No. **105**:

There is **no shame** in **rum raisin** ice cream.

Rule No. 106:

Yams are the most under-appreciated tuber.

Rule No. 107:

Beau is the most under-appreciated Bridges.

Rule No. 108:

No movie should have its title incorporated into the dialogue.

Rule No. 109:

Unless you are a Pilgrim, large shoe buckles are to be avoided.

Rule No. **110**:

Never trust anyone with a home **phone** number that ends in **00**.

Rule No. **112**:

Tollbooths are not for the **asking** of. **directions**.

Rule No. **111**:

The **stupider** the man, the **slower** he walks.

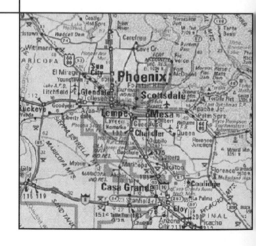

Rule No. 113:

The best blind dates are with girls named Kelly or Samantha.

Rule No. 114:

White basketball players should be extraordinarily white and should have bad hair.

Rule No. 115:

Foreigner is playing at a small venue near you tonight. And tickets are still available.

Rule No. **116**:

Words that end in **"oma"** (e.g., melanoma) are **bad**.

Rule No. **117**:

Words that end in **"iti"**, **"ita"**, or **"ata"** (e.g., ziti, margarita, frittata) are just plain **delicious**.

Rule No. **118**:

Your **car** never runs **better**, **faster**, or **smoother** than just after it's **washed**.

Rule No. 119:

Trust no one who uses unusual paper clips.

Rule No. 120:

Fried calamari is invariably disappointing.

Rule No. 121:

Gratuitous nazi-bashing never goes out of style.

Rule No. 122:

Nobody named "Josh" is over 35.

Rule No. 124:

People with alliterative first and last names aren't in on the joke.

Rule No. 123:

Hip Asians are hipper than people from any other ethnic group.

Rule No. 125:

When it comes to personalized stationery, men don't have it.

Rule No. 126:

Never trust a man who uses a vibrato while singing "Happy Birthday."

Rule No. 127:

There is nothing funnier than cussing puppets.

Rule No. **128**:

When in doubt,
go bowling.

Rule No. **129**:

There is **so much**
a **mustache**
says about a man.

Rule No. **130**:

And **none** of it
is **good**.

Rule No. 131:

Slow-motion violence goes best with the work of Gustav Mahler.

Rule No. 132:

Be wary of people who address their dad as "Father."

Rule No. 133:

Be even more wary of people who address their dad as "Colonel."

Rule No. 134:

Every great poet has, at least once, described the ocean as undulating.

Rule No. 135:

A man should avoid using the phrase "assume the position" on the first date.

Rule No. 136:

A papasan chair is discarded in the United States every 7.5 seconds.

Rule No. **137**:

Doric
are
the best
columns.

Rule No. **138**:

Anyone who reads
the *Hollywood
Reporter*
in public is a
jackass.

Rule No. **139**:

Chest hair will be
back in style
by autumn
2010.

Rule No. 140:

The study of plate tectonics is best left to professionals.

Rule No. 141:

All directors named Todd are critically acclaimed.

Rule No. 142:

You will make friends by jumping on the anti-Andrew Lloyd Webber bandwagon.

Rule No. **143**:

Never begin an **essay** with a **quote** from the **Bible**.

Rule No. **144**:

Especially **Deuteronomy**.

Rule No. **145**:

Wishing we were still **united** in a **supercontinent** known as **Pangaea** is not the **best** use of your **time**.

Rule No. 146:

The best vowel modifier is the umlaut.

Rule No. 148:

Or after a body of water.

Rule No. 147:

Never name a child after a continent, a nation, or a commonwealth.

Rule No. 149:

Especially if that body of water is a canal.

Rule No. 151:

Or whose father calls her "butch."

Rule No. 150:

Never date a woman whose father calls her "princess."

Rule No. **152**:

More
nougat.

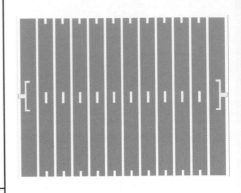

Rule No. **153**:

If someone begins an opinion by saying, "Now, I'm not [fill in the blank]," then that person is "[fill in the blank]."

Rule No. **154**:

The best shape is the rectangle.

Rule No. **155**:

No straws.

Rule No. **156**:

People who use the word "classy" aren't.

Rule No. **157**:

The only time it's acceptable for a man to shut one eye is when he's taking a picture.

Rule No. 158:

The comma and the colon are the only acceptable punctuation in movie titles.

Rule No. 159:

"Partner" is a noun, not a verb.

Rule No. 160:

The future has no buttons.

Rule No. 161:

Not nearly enough guys are named Remus.

Rule No. 162:

You can't think of the Gutenberg Bible without thinking of Steve.

Rule No. 163:

Spanish-speaking people can call New York "Nueva York," but English-speaking people can't call Puerto Rico "Richport."

Rule No. **164**:

The people who **choose** to be **nudists** are **never** the people you **wish to be** nudists.

Rule No. **166**:

Loofahs for everyone!

Rule No. **165**:

The people who **elect** to perform **karaoke** are **never** the people you wish would **perform** karaoke.

Rule No. **167**:

Never confer on the creepy **habits** of the tech-support guy via e-mail.

Rule No. **168**:

You can't meet a **man** named "**Colin**," as in Powell, without thinking, "Well, he **could have been** named '**Bunghole**.'"

Rule No. **169**:

You **cut** the **fat**, you **cut** the **flavor**.

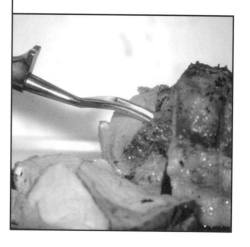

Rule No. 170:

Laundry activity shall be outsourced whenever possible.

Rule No. 171:

Woodward is to Bernstein as Cher is to Sonny.

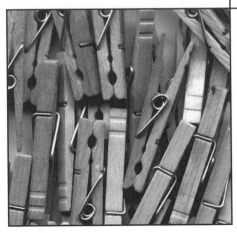

Rule No. 172:

Mayonnaise and Dijon mustard are to be combined on a case-by-case basis.

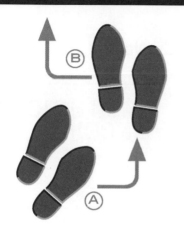

Rule No. 173:

White men with lots of **college** look the **funniest** when dancing.

Rule No. 174:

The only thing **stupider** than the names of **hair salons** are the names people give their **boats**. (May we draw your **attention** to the **inordinate** number of **speedboats** called "Wet Dream.")

Rule No. **175**:

No one finds out you're a tea drinker until after you've got the job.

Rule No. **176**:

The best instrument is the cello.

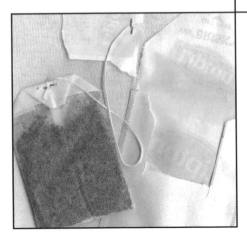

Rule No. **177**:

Marisa Tomei is to Todd Rundgren as Susan Faludi is to Boutros Boutros-Ghali.

Rule No. 178:

Cairo is the nicest city with open sewers.

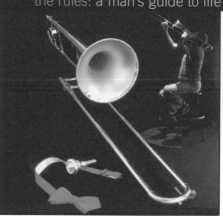

Rule No. 179:

You don't know anyone named Natasha.

Rule No. 180:

Television actors who are also musicians get plotlines that allow them to demonstrate this musical talent on their shows.

Rule No. 181:

Women dig
preachers.

Rule No. 182:

No one
will ever tell you
that the chicken
salad was
not made today.

Rule No. 183:

Light a
cigarette
and your dinner
will arrive.

Rule No. 184:

Leaders of religions get larger houses and better cars than followers of religions.

Rule No. 185:

Girl Scout cookies are for buying, not eating.

Rule No. 186:

Although a failed business is correctly described as "defunct," it does not follow that a going concern is "funct."

Rule No. 187:

There is no shame in well-done steak.

Rule No. 188:

Always keep your receipt from RadioShack.

Rule No. 189:

The roles Teri Garr used to get now go to Lisa Kudrow.

Rule No. 190:

You're not supposed to like your job.

Rule No. 191:

Men named **Walter** are taken **more seriously** than men named **Jason**. Also **Billy**.

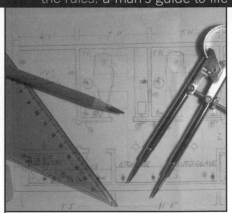

Rule No. 192:

Female **pastry chefs** are to men as male **architects** are to women.

Rule No. **193**:

It's always **time** for pie!

Rule No. **194**:

Cranberry sauce is a **perfectly good condiment** the other **364** days of the year, too.

Rule No. **195**:

Religion causes some people to get **really angry** and others to **grow** long, funny **beards**.

Rule No. **196**:

Making a living as a man who turns into a huge green monster with tight, tattered pants to fight crime is fine and dandy – it's your choice. But know this: It's a lonely, lonely life.

Rule No. **197**:

Executives, don't need presents.

Rule No. **198**:

Don't fuck with broccoli.

Rule No. **199**:

You don't have to be a football hero to get along with beautiful girls. Arab princes do okay. Also, short guys with a lot of money.

Rule No. **200**:

There is nothing that can be marketed that cannot be better marketed using the likeness of Honest Abe Lincoln.

Rule No. **201**:

People named Gil
never
win
awards.

Rule No. **202**:

Investing in
faraway **banana**
republics with
worthless currencies,
dubious infrastructures,
and heavily armed
police **is risky**.

Rule No. **203**:

The **best looking**
musician is always
the **lead**
singer,
followed in
descending order
by the **lead**
guitarist,
rhythm
guitarist,
drummer, and
bass player.

Rule No. **204**:

There are words to say when playing touch football. "Got you" is fine. "Touchdown," expected. But "Hey, too hard!" – that's a no-no.

Rule No. **205**:

The man who wears a bunny suit is a greater man than the one who wears a business suit.

Rule No. **206**:

When intellectuals are "white, they're called intellectuals." When they're black, they're called "black intellectuals."

Rule No. 207:

The only thing better than a huge, rich company is when a huger, richer company buys it and afterward the CEOs shake hands. They seem so happy that it's kind of contagious.

Rule No. 208:

If there's one thing that comes out of a terrible tragedy, it's really dumb legislation.

Rule No. 209:

It's interesting to hear, about directors' battles with studio executives. Darned studio executives!

Rule No. 210:

The best religions have great hats.

Rule No. 211:

Crazy men are to be played by Dennis Hopper. Weird men are to be played by Steve Buscemi.

Rule No. 212:

The little extra you pay for name-brand tin foil is well worth it.

Rule No. 213:

Pompous people like to be called pompous.

Rule No. 214:

The last people who should be having kids are always the first to do so.

Rule No. 215:

Those who enjoy musical theater should ask themselves, for their own sake and that of their countrymen, "Why?"

Rule No. **216**:

When you have a headache and you are tired and you have not slept for forty-six hours and will not sleep for eight more, people will talk louder, and in Arabic.

Rule No. **217**:

Melon should be more popular.

Rule No. **218**:

Yes, seat belts do wrinkle your suit, but so do windshields.

Rule No. **219**:

There is no shame in grape soda.

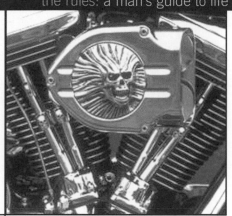

Rule No. **220**:

You are not on the team that plays in your city. They are not "we"; their wins are not yours.

Rule No. **221**:

A motorcyclist, even an Irish motorcyclist, does not want to hear, "May the road always rise to meet you."

Rule No. **222**:

Some **women,** particularly **models,** "call one another "**girls,**" but you can't.

Rule No. **223**:

The savvy, punctual carpool **driver** does not offer **travel mug** coffee to the **guy** who always has to **pee.**

Rule No. **224**:

People eager to get **married** can be **trusted** about as much as people eager to get **elected.**

Rule No. **225**:

For a multitude
of reasons,
tanned people
are not to be
trusted.

Rule No. **227**:

It's okay to be
friendly
to cops.

Rule No. **226**:

Laugh at your
enemies.
It couldn't
possibly make
things worse.

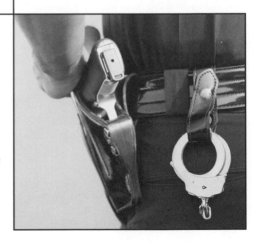

Rule No. **228**:

People who **fish** are very **different** from people who **don't fish.**

Rule No. **229**:

There is **nothing good** about **berets.**

Rule No. **230**:

No **woman** over the **age** of **17** has ever been **thrilled** by the gift of **carnations.**

Rule No. **231**:

It's okay to lie to liars.

Rule No. **232**:

It's not what you wear or how you wear it or when you bought it or who else has it. It's what it cost.

Rule No. **233**:

It's not who you know but how you know them – and how many other people know who you know and how you know them. Also helpful: pictures to prove it.

Rule No. 234:

The **sexiest** fruit is the **fig**, followed by the **peach**, the **plum**, and the **pomegranate**.

Rule No. 235:

The **least sexy** fruit: the **Frankenberry**.

Rule No. 236:

Big men **sail** **little** boats.

Rule No. 237:

It is always unacceptable to refuse a woman's request to dance.

Rule No. 238:

Especially when she is your mother's age.

Rule No. 239:

More especially when she is your mother.

Rule No. **240**:

In the **parlance** of **real** estate professionals, **plants** are called "**plant materials**."

Rule No. **241**:

In the parlance of **airline-industry** professionals, cigarettes are called "**smoking materials**."

Rule No. **242**:

In the parlance of **fashion-industry** professionals, a pair of **pants** is called "**a pant**."

Rule No. 243:

To make it really big on the radio you need a nickname along the lines of Cletus the Fetus.

Rule No. 244:

This does not apply to National Public Radio.

Rule No. 245:

Never go home with a woman who smokes cigarillos.

Rule No. 246:

People who call ping-pong "table tennis" will always beat you.

Rule No. **247**:

Any word employed as a prefix for the word "pants" results in a word that is funny, e.g., finicky-pants, funkypants, happypants, googlypants, nancypants, and boogly-booglypants.

Rule No. **248**:

Except for disestablish-mentarianism-pants. Not funny.

Rule No. **249**:

The best number is 7, followed closely by 9.

Rule No. 250:

There is no worst number; all others are of equal merit.

Rule No. 252:

But stubborn people are always more effective.

Rule No. 251:

Pliant people are, more often than not, smarter than stubborn people.

Rule No. 253:

If a Halloween costume is unavoidable, it must preserve your good looks, involve no makeup, and be quickly removed in the event of passion.

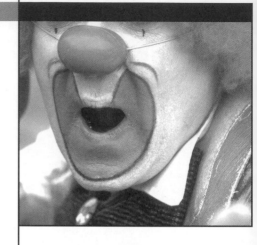

Rule No. 254:

Because even smiling clowns are scary.

Rule No. 255:

And the guy in the gorilla suit gets sweaty, not lucky.

Rule No. 256:

The fatter the man, the smaller the swimsuit.

Rule No. 257:

Satan loves parents who give young children rat-tail haircuts.

Rule No. 258:

Satan loves parents who dress young children in leather jackets and shades.

Rule No. **259**:

The absolute **maximum** number of times that you can **quote** Monty **Python** on a first **date** and still have a reasonable **expectation** of getting **laid** is: **zero.**

Rule No. **260**:

It's **okay** if you're **overweight.**

Rule No. **261**:

As long as you can **dance.**

Rule No. **262**:

If a man is **wearing** a **class ring,** do not **respect** him.

Rule No. **263**:

If a man is **wearing** a **pinky ring,** do not **fuck** with him.

Rule No. **264**:

If a man is **wearing** a ring with the **papal insignia** on it, then he is the **Pope,** and try not to **curse** in front of him.

Rule No. 265:

Self-cleaning
ovens
usually aren't.

Rule No. 266:

Scrub-free
cleansing
products
never are.

Rule No. 267:

Wrinkle-
resistant
trousers,
oddly, actually
do resist
wrinkles.
Unfortunately,
they also
resist the
opposite sex.

Rule No. 269:

On any road trip, he who is driving gets control of the radio. No exceptions.

Rule No. 268:

Before getting any sort of tattoo, devote a few minutes' thought to how it will look on your saggy wrinkled flesh in the nursing home.

Rule No. 270:

Well, if he who is driving is a really big fan of Celine Dion, there should at least be some sort of negotiation.

Rule No. **271**:

No man can own a longhaired cat and still command respect.

Rule No. **272**:

Even the very best "gentlemen's clubs" feel a little bit like sad, sad zoos.

Rule No. **273**:

Even the very best zoos feel a little bit like animal prisons.

Rule No. 274:

Certainly, it is your prerogative to be difficult in restaurants. Just as it's a restaurant worker's prerogative to place unwanted fluids in your meal.

Rule No. 275:

No ponytail, unless you are Willie Nelson.

Rule No. 276:

If you are uncertain how much cologne is enough, you are not allowed to use cologne.

Rule No. 277:

The quickest way to impress twins is to be able to figure out which is which.

Rule No. 278:

The quickest way to impress triplets is to not spend ten minutes discussing the fact that they're triplets.

Rule No. 279:

The correct description for any photograph of someone else's baby is "adorable." Have this word ready to go before the photograph is shown, so that, even if the baby is shockingly ugly, you can utter "adorable" without hesitation.

Rule No. 280:

In cars and pets, selecting the fashionable one of the moment is always, always a mistake. (Unless you enjoy riding around in your Hummer with your Vietnamese potbellied pig.)

Rule No. 281:

Anyone who defends their opinion with, ".Well, it's my opinion, and I'm entitled to it," should be taken out and shot.

Rule No. 282:

When meeting new people: The first name terminating in an "i" is strike one. Dotting the "i" with a heart is strike two. And if it's a guy, that's strike three.

Rule No. 283:

There is no shame in milk and cookies.

Rule No. 284:

A complicated coffee order impresses no one.

Rule No. 285:

Never wave at a video camera.

Rule No. 286:

The words "Bruckheimer" and "first date" do not belong in the same sentence.

Rule No. 287:

The words "dirt cheap" and "sushi" do not belong in the same sentence—or, rather, if they are in the same sentence, that sentence also often includes "intestinal parasite."

Rule No. **288**:

"Irregardless" is
not a word,
irregardless
of what you say.

Rule No. **289**:

If you're **making** a
sign to be held up
at a sporting **event**,
it doesn't hurt
to **use** a
dictionary.

Rule No. **290**:

When someone
sneezes four
times in **rapid-**
fire succession,
one
"Bless You"
will suffice.

Rule No. 291:

There is
no shame
in eggs
for dinner.

Rule No. 292:

There is
no shame
in cinnamon
toast.

Rule No. 293:

There is, however,
ample shame
in eating a
Lean Cuisine
entrée at home,
alone, pantless,
while watching
television.
Look at
yourself, man.
Just look
at yourself.

Rule No. **294**:

Harvard
Extension is
NOT
Harvard.

Rule No. **295**:

Never select
a tattoo
just because it's
on sale.

Rule No. **296**:

You really need
closer to two
apples a day
now to keep
the doctor
away.

Rule No. **297**:

There's **no need** to thank someone for their **"thank you"** card.

Rule No. **299**:

A **muffin** is just cake in the **shape** of a **mushroom**.

Rule No. **298**:

If you're under **80**, you should **never** utter the phrase "the whole **kit** and **kaboodle**."

Rule No. **300**:

A **power bar** is just a candy bar in a **shiny wrapper**.

Rule No. **301**:

If something has **raisins** in it, they have to be **mentioned in** its **name**.

Rule No. **302**:

It's **tough** to find a great **harmonica teacher**.

Rule No. **303**:

The **weirder** the cell phone **ring**, the more **annoying** the **person**.

Rule No. **304**:

Jewish comics
are **really**
funny in their
twenties, thirties
and forties,
not so
funny in
their fifties and
sixties, and then
hilarious in
their seventies.

Rule No. **305**:

Your child is only
38% as cute
as you think
he is.

Rule No. **306**:

If your second
toe is bigger
than your first toe
you don't have
to wait in lines
anymore.

Rule No. 307:

Here is how movies work: They are filmed on soundstages in California, and then they are edited and duplicated, and then, months later, they are shipped in canisters to your local multiplex.

Rule No. 308:

All of which tends to suggest that, when you yell at the heroine on screen, she cannot hear you, no matter how loud you yell, or how important your instructions are to her personal safety.

Rule No. 309:

Similarly, if you find yourself really enjoying a movie, and are moved to applaud when it is over, ask yourself: "What the fuck am I doing?"

Rule No. 310:

Being a regular at Starbucks is nothing to brag about.

Rule No. 311:

Some chicken doesn't even taste like chicken.

Rule No. **312**:

All bottled water comes from a faucet in Richmond.

Rule No. **313**:

If you still cook on a hot plate at home it's not gonna be easy getting that car loan.

Rule No. **314**:

There's no reason to ever say "whoops" out loud.

Rule No. 315:

Being a coal miner is tougher than being a coal miner's daughter.

Rule No. 316:

Quentin is to Tarantino as one-hit is to wonder.

Rule No. 317:

Orange marmalade does not qualify as jam.

Rule No. 318:

Don't **wear** anything with **#1** on it, unless you happen to be **Tony** Fernandez or **Lance** Johnson.

Rule No. 319:

Less than 1% of **dentists** are **funny.**

Rule No. 320:

Your bank **pin** number should **never** be your **birthday.**

Rule No. 321:

On forms where it says "sex," and you write "yes!" they have the right to crumple up your document and fire rubber bullets at your groin.

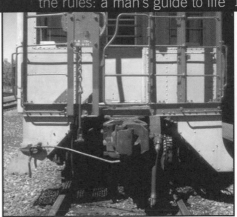

Rule No. 322:

Women who tie sweaters around their waists have big asses.

Rule No. 323:

Food tastes immeasurably better on the barbecue if you light the fire with those "Don't Sweat the Small Stuff" books.

Rule No. 324:

You know you've made it when there's a bobblehead doll of you.

Rule No. **325**:

Among the emotions it is impossible to maintain plausibly while wearing leopard-skin clothing: stoicism, ferocity, dourness, studiousness.'

Rule No. **326**:

Wear no leopard-skin clothing. No, not even there.

Rule No. **327**:

Having a ferret as a pet doesn't make you any cooler. In fact, it actually makes the ferret less cool.

Rule No. 328:

Any superhero worth his salt could fly without his cape.

Rule No. 329:

If your head's at the proper angle, smoking actually does make you look cool.

Rule No. 330:

You should never be subjected to looking at a man's toes.

Rule No. 331:

No one should be arrested for keying a car with a vanity plate.

Rule No. **332**:

People who used to **follow** the Grateful Dead across the country are **really** bored now.

Rule No. **333**:

They were **bored then,** too.

Rule No. **334**:

"We Will Rock You" is the **dumbest** sports anthem song **ever.**

Rule No. 335:

Walking into **Staples** and shouting, "Hey, **where** are the **staples**?" isn't funny.

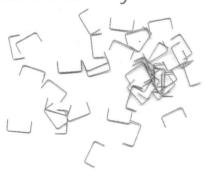

Rule No. 336:

Captain Crunch should be Admiral Crunch by now.

Rule No. 337:

High-fiving another man at a restaurant could very well be the **reason** you're **single**.

Rule No. **338**:

Pennies are inappropriate at strip clubs.

Rule No. **340**:

Teenagers with aggressively asymmetrical hair get beat up a lot.

Rule No. **339**:

Dogs with bandannas tied around their necks are not pleased with the accessory.

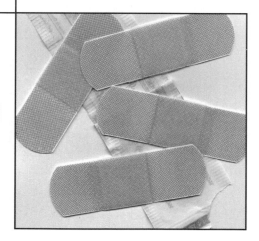

Rule No. **341**:

Do not give yourself a nickname.

Rule No. **343**:

No fluorescent condoms, unless they're all that's available.

Rule No. **342**:

Do not make up your own catchphrase.

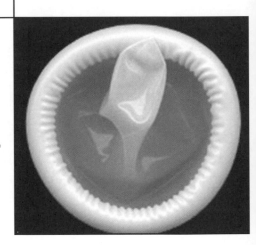

Rule No. **344**:

You will actually be **rewarded** in the **afterlife** for **re-gifting**.

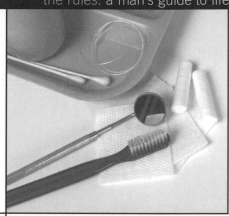

Rule No. **345**:

Law firm **quality**, in descending **order: two** names, **four** names, **three** names, **one** name, **five** names.

Rule No. **346**:

If Steve **Buscemi** got his **teeth fixed** he'd probably **never work** again.

Rule No. **347**:

Do not **argue** with the **caricaturist.**

Rule No. **348**:

Midget humor is overrated, **monkey** humor is underrated.

Rule No. **349**:

Ninety-seven percent of **hockey nicknames** are created by adding an **"ee"** sound to a player's **last name.**

Rule No. 350:

All swimsuit models must complain about shoot conditions in the "making of" documentaries.

Rule No. 351:

Americans who say "cheers" are pretentious twits.

Rule No. 352:

First class is to business class is to coach as Groucho is to Harpo is to Zeppo.

Rule No. 353:

No one likes audiophiles —even other audiophiles.

Rule No. 354:

Trendy names only if you know your kid is going to be cute.

Rule No. 355:

A woman's chin and knees are the most underrated parts of her body.

Rule No. **356**:

Jokes about golf clothes are more passé than the clothes.

Rule No. **357**:

Except on the golf course, golf umbrellas are unmanly.

Rule No. **358**:

Try the brisket.

Rule No. **359**:

Women who have **two** or more brothers are **less likely** to be disgusted by you.

Rule No. **360**:

Hat-brim **bending decreases** with age.

Rule No. **361**:

Women who **come** from **big** families are **more fun**.

Rule No. 362:

Character actors have big ears.

Rule No. 364:

Bald umpires are excellent, no matter the sport.

Rule No. 363:

Pigeon-toed people are quicker than splay-footed people.

Rule No. 365:

You'll live to regret trading in those CDs, except for the Spin Doctors.

Rule No. **366**:

That new Bob Dylan album isn't quite as good as everyone says it is.

Rule No. **367**:

That new Woody Allen film is worse than everyone says it is.

Rule No. **368**:

Soda tastes 27 percent better from glass bottles than plastic; wine, 79 percent.

Rule No. 370:

Avoid restaurants that serve both Chinese and Japanese food.

Rule No. 369:

Nobody comes to watch the coach, no matter what he may think.

Rule No. 371:

She looks cute tucking her hair behind her ears; you look ridiculous.

Rule No. **372**:

When
in doubt,
pick "C."

Rule No. **373**:

Sinatra is
never wrong.

Rule No. **374**:

Minor league
ballparks
serve the
best
hot dogs.

Rule No. 375:

Do not quote Bryan Adams' songs, even ironically.

Rule No. 376:

No cameras at the bachelor party, and definitely no video cameras.

Rule No. 377:

If it bends, it's funny. If it bends two ways, it's even funnier. If it bends three ways, marry it.

Rule No. **378**:

From one dude to another: enough with the "dude" already.

Rule No. **379**:

In descending order: a tad, a soupçon, a smidge.

Rule No. **380**:

Sophisticated though it may be, you can't say "sipping whiskey" without feeling goofy.

Rule No. 381:

History is told by the winners, oral histories are told by old men eating tuna-fish sandwiches in the park.

Rule No. 382:

Being hung in effigy is not a backhanded compliment.

Rule No. 383:

The History Channel is not a substitute for reading a book every now and then.

Rule No. **384**:

Diplomas are not for framing.

Rule No. **385**:

Calling the phone numbers cited in movies or plays will not give you entrée into their fictional worlds.

Rule No. **386**:

O Brother, Where Art Thou? was great. But playing scratchy WPA tapes of guys with three teeth and a junkyard washboard while driving your Lexus RX doesn't actually make you authentically rootsy.

Rule No. **387**:

There's no
historical
basis for
Count
Chocula.

Rule No. **389**:

Fishnet stockings
made from
actual fishnets
aren't all that
sexy.

Rule No. **388**:

There's a special
circle in Hell
reserved for those who
adjust their
rearview mirrors
while you wait for
their parking space.

Rule No. 390:

If you **wonder,** even momentarily, about the **toilet** and shower facilities at **Burning Man,** you're **too old** to attend.

Rule No. 391:

Never mind what time it is, **never pose** for a **"zany"** snapshot **squatting** over Old **Faithful.**

Rule No. 392:

The French horn at the very beginning of "You Can't Always Get What You Want" is rock's best use of that instrument.

Rule No. 393:

A man wearing a brightly colored fanny pack is 7/8th of a man.

Rule No. 394:

As miserable mental illnesses go, manic-depressive just sounds better than bi-polar.

Rule No. **395**:

A gentleman **never** considers **sexual activity** until the **dog** has been **sent** to another room.

Rule No. **396**:

Especially if it's a **Jack Russell** terrier **or** could be related to **Marmaduke**.

Rule No. **397**:

A man **wearing** a **paper** trainee **hat** is, during the **time** he has it on, **precisely 1/6th** of a **man**.

Rule No. **399**:

A first-date restaurant should never feature an all-you-can-eat salad bar.

Rule No. **398**:

Never attempt "this really cool thing I saw on Animal Planet / Crocodile Hunter / The X Games."

Rule No. **400**:

Never trust a man with more than one umlaut in his name.

Rule No. 401:

Reaching over to flush another man's urinal is universally frowned upon.

Rule No. 402:

You will never meet a woman named Rapunzel.

Rule No. 403:

If you do, she'll have the shortest, butchiest haircut imaginable.

Rule No. **404**:

Explaining how your **shoes** came to be called, "**wingtips**" will **not** get you **laid**.

Rule No. **405**:

By now, in **all fairness**, it should be called Lou **Gehrig's** and Stephen **Hawking's** disease.

Rule No. **406**:

Any **recipe** requiring **cumin** is nothing but **hoop-jumping** bullshit.

Rule No. 407:

Asking her if you can come up "just to use your bathroom," is the Hail Mary pass of romantic moves.

Rule No. 409:

Agreeing to date other people "for now," is the punt-on-third-down of romantic moves.

Rule No. 408:

Agreeing to "take things slow" is the deep-drop screen pass of romantic moves.

Rule No. **410**:

Pretending to conduct an orchestra playing the *Mission Impossible* theme song will not get you laid.

Rule No. **411**:

It's okay to die never knowing how electric eels mate without stunning one another.

Rule No. **412**:

Any man who'd participate in an X-rated version of the Hokey Pokey is 3/16ths of a man.

Rule No. **413**:

It's **never okay** to build or obsessively visit a **web** site **shrine** to someone featured in an **Apple** ad.

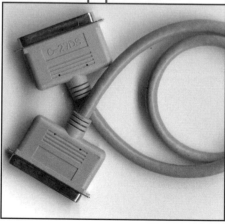

Rule No. **414**:

If you're **consuming** something to **flavor** your **semen** your life has **devolved** into nothing but a series of **tawdry** minor amusements.

Rule No. 415:

At the checkout counter on your third date, if she says, "Oh wait, we're gonna need chocolate syrup," don't ask what for, just go get it.

Rule No. 416:

Pretending to get all confused in the elevator and pressing her nipple instead of a floor button will not get you laid.

Rule No. 417:

Never discuss **affairs** of the **heart** with a guy who refers to sexual **intimacy** as "my daily **requirement** of **vitamin F."**

Rule No. 418:

It's **not okay** to be in a **tribute** band to **another** **tribute** band.

Rule No. 419:

Your **Etch-a-Sketch** portraits of notable, politicians **won't** get you **laid.**

Rule No. **420**:

You are absolutely the **only person calling** during that PBS **pledge break.** Every other **penny** comes from the **John** D. and **Catherine** T. **MacArthur Foundation,** and the **Chubb Group** of Insurance Companies.

Rule No. **421**:

"Before" models are more **likely** to **respond** to fan mail.

Rule No. 422:

If you live long enough you will resemble a gargoyle.

Rule No. 423:

Only musicians have chops.

Rule No. 424:

But it would be nice if actuaries could have them too.

Rule No. 425:

The day that the *New York Times* referred to Snoop Doggy Dogg on second reference as Mr. Dogg was the day the whole formal news outlet edifice began to crumble.

Rule No. 426:

Explaining why Tesla was actually more brilliant than Edison won't get you laid.

Rule No. 427:

Full frontal nudity isn't necessarily sexier than nudity seen from the side.

Rule No. 428:

Nobody should name their kids after Melville characters: Not Ishmael. Not Ahab. Not Bartleby. Not Queeqegg. Not Tashetego. Not Daggoo. Not Radney. Not Fedallah. Not Mayhew.

Rule No. 429:

Effigies don't have to be anatomically correct as long as they're flammable.

Rule No. 430:

The hottest funk-and-soul metaphors for beautiful women are, in descending order: Brick-houuuse! Little red corvette. Once-twice-three-times a lady.

Rule No. 431:

Never let a motion picture from a trans-global media conglomerate that's been test-marketed and had several scenes re-shot to hone its appeal for key target demographics touch your very soul.

Rule No. **432**:

At the **holiday** office party, **consume** one drink **less** than your **boss.**

Rule No. **433**:

Every man should know how to **make** at least **one drink** from a **foreign** country, preferably one **taught** to him by a local **female** with whom he has had a **complicated,** unresolved, and **quite** possibly **dangerous dalliance.**

Rule No. 434:

There is rarely any **genuine** need to shout "Skäl!" "Na zdorovye!" "Sláinte!" "Bottoms up!" or "Down the hatch!"

Rule No. 435:

There is **no upside** to karaoke.

Rule No. 436:

There is an **ever-so-slight** upside to a **wet T-shirt contest,** as long as you're **not** in it.

Rule No. 437:

Condoms that are red or green or any color but clear will make your manly bits appear to be red or green.

Rule No. 438:

A relaxed dress code at work does not legitimize the display of leg hair or chest hair.

Rule No. 439:

To foster its use in your home, call it erotica, not porn.

Rule No. 440:

Shorts in the office: only if your office is a wooden chair mounted atop a ladder on a sunny beach and a whistle hangs from around your neck.

Rule No. 441:

Never utter the words I and love and you if you've had more than three drinks.

Rule No. **442**:

Only acceptable pick-up line: "Hi, my name is [insert your name], What's yours?"

Rule No. **443**:

Women like a man who likes women who like to eat.

Rule No. **444**:

Self-expression is not achieved via cartoon-character ties or watches, unless the expression one wishes to achieve is: "loser."

Rule No. **445**:

No matter how furtive or quick the glance, a woman always knows when you're looking at her breasts.

Rule No. **446**:

Love does **not** mean never having to **say** you're **sorry.** It means **having** to say you're sorry **over** and **over** again, in **new** and different **ways,** **every** day, **every** week, **every** month, even when you **don't want to,** **every** year, until God grants you his **mercy** and you finally, blissfully **die.**

Rule No. **447**:

The only thing **more important** than saying "**No**, you don't **look fat** in that outfit" when she **asks** you the first time, is the deep **sincerity** with which you must say "**Really**" when she asks the **second** time.

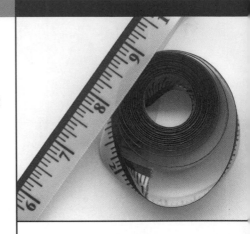

Rule No. **448**:

If you **ask** about her previous **boyfriend** and she gets a small, **wistful smile** on her face, **change** the subject.

Rule No. **449**:

Know that while **Rhett Butler** can get away with telling **Scarlett O'Hara** that she "should be **kissed,** and **often,** and by someone who **knows how,**" you cannot.

Rule No. **450**:

If you're **single,** the **tango** will do the **trick.** If you're **married,** the **tango** will also do the **trick.** **Possibly** even **with** your **wife.**

Rule No. **451**:

It is important to avoid rhyming sexual innuendoes such as "urge to merge."

Rule No. **452**:

And especially "inclination towards copulation."

Rule No. **453**:

Never trust a man wearing a Lakers jersey, a Clippers hat, and a Raiders jacket all at once.

Rule No. **454**:

People who begin sentences by **saying,** "With all **due** respect," are in fact preparing to impart **loads** of disrespect.

Rule No. **455**:

If a **young boy** asks you to tell him a **story,** simply include a **house** with **secret passageways** and his **satisfaction** will be immediate.

Rule No. 456:

There are few things **sadder** than a man over **40** playing **air guitar.**

Rule No. 458:

"That's **what she said"** jokes from men over **40** are only moderately less **sad** than **air guitar.**

Rule No. 457:

While out on a **"buddies** only" getaway, **93** percent of all statements can be **turned** into a "That's **what she said",** joke.

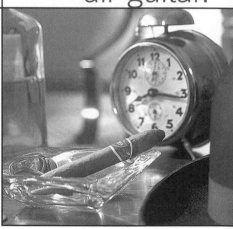

Rule No. **459**:

Never trust a man who knows all the dance **steps** to "Bye, Bye, Bye."

Rule No. **460**:

Never trust a man who **owns** a **video** of his middle **school** musical.

Rule No. **461**:

Every man should **buy** a **round** for an **entire bar** at least **once** in his **life**.

Rule No. **462**:

When the frost is on the pumpkin, it's time for dicky dunkin'.

Rule No. **463**:

When it's hot and sticky, it's not time for dunkin' dicky.

Rule No. **464**:

The reverse in each case is equally true. Use as required.

Rule No. **465**:

No **short** man was **ever** named Orlando.

Rule No. **466**:

The lower you **wear** your **bass guitar,** the **cooler** you are.

Rule No. **467**:

When a **girlfriend** and a **mouse** are in the same **room,** a man does **not belong** on the chair.

Rule No. **468**:

Never order a sloppy Joe on a first date.

Rule No. **469**:

A man over the age of 30 should not make innuendoes about things that happen to involve the number 69.

Rule No. **470**:

If your dream involves an elaborate plot in which you are looking for a bathroom, it's time to get up and take a pee.

Rule No. 471:

Any actor who uses the word "craft" to refer to acting should be the subject of a public flogging.

Rule No. 472:

Go ahead. Be a vegan. All we ask is that you do so quietly.

Rule No. 473:

You should never spend more than $20 on a pen.

Rule No. 474:

Asking "Who had the steak and who had the fish?" is not the manly way to go about paying for dinner.

Rule No. 475:

There's no thrill like the thrill of getting cash in the mail.

Rule No. 476:

A bath in the movies requires at minimum eight candles near the bathtub.

Rule No. 477:

Nobody cares about your dreams.

Rule No. 479:

Conversely, the best color for a new ski boat is red.

Rule No. 478:

The worst color for a new car is red.

Rule No. 480:

If there is danger involved, it is fun.

Rule No. 481:

It is more fun if it requires you to sign a waiver.

Rule No. 482:

Practicing half-court shots becomes unacceptable after the age of 14.

Rule No. **483**:

When a joke is immediately followed by the phrase "Get it?", the joke's potential comedic value drops by an estimated 80 percent.

Rule No. **484**:

The best mogul name ever is T. Boone Pickens.

Rule No. **485**:

The response "you are" is no longer acceptable as a response for the question "what's happening?"

Rule No. **486**:

A man over the age of 30 should never read a book with the words "Zen and the Art of" in the title.

Rule No. **487**:

A man over the age of 30 should not own a futon or a beanbag chair.

Rule No. **488**:

A man over the age of 30 should not use the word "Dawg" except to refer to a creature with four legs and a leash around its neck.

Rule No. **489**:

A man **over** the **age** of **30** should not refer to breasts as "**chesticles**."

Rule No. **490**:

A man **over** the **age** of **30** should never do impressions of **Austin Powers** characters, most especially **Fat Bastard**.

Rule No. **491**:

A man **over** the **age** of **30** should not pick a **fistfight** by **thrusting** out his **neck**, **flexing**, and screaming "It's **go** time!" to passersby.

Rule No. 492:

A restaurant that **charges** a **surcharge** for blue cheese **dressing** is a restaurant to **stay** far **away** from.

Rule No. 493:

Scoreboard "**races**" demean us all.

Rule No. 494:

But **always** bet on **green**.

Rule No. **495**:

If you are a **movie character** in a **hurry** and are driving through a **rural** area, you will run into a **herd** of **sheep** **crossing** the road.

Rule No. **496**:

Condiments should **not** be the subject of **media** publicity campaigns.

Rule No. 497:

Ketchup is back in!

Rule No. 498:

Oddly, both of the following statements are true: Monkeys are never funnier than when they're wearing clothing. And monkeys are never sadder than when they're wearing clothing.

Rule No. 499:

The best way to get out of a bad date is to claim that you own a ferret.

Rule No. 500:

Unless, of course, your date excitedly says that she, too, owns a ferret.

Rule No. 501:

Nobody on a political talk show has ever convinced a fellow panelist of anything. Never happened, never will.

Rule No. 502:

The appeal of the small, non-corporate, independently owned and operated coffeehouse usually lasts right up until the moment you taste the coffee.

Rule No. 503:

Every dish can be improved with the addition of bacon.

Rule No. 504:

The slower the movie, the better the reviews.

Rule No. 505:

Women whose names end with the letter "i" are more promiscuous.

Rule No. 506:

A man can never own too many pairs of socks.

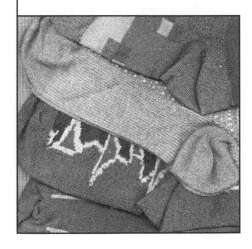

Rule No. **507**:

There is **nothing worse** than a **white guy** who **wants** to be a Native American.

Rule No. **508**:

When **in doubt,** give something in a **pale blue** box.

Rule No. **509**:

Mexican restaurants have the **worst** red **wine.**

Rule No. 511:

The **worst** cat **name** is anything beginning with "Mister."

Rule No. 510:

The **best** dog **name** is "Rex."

Rule No. 512:

Three out of every **four** short-order **cooks** have served **jail time.**

Rule No. **513**:

People who live in glass houses watch **65** percent less porn.

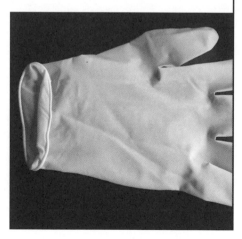

Rule No. **514**:

After dinner, when you reach into your wallet a little more slowly than everyone else, trust us, they all notice.

Rule No. 515:

A self-respecting man should not know how to say anything in Klingon.

Rule No. 516:

A self-respecting man should not know how to say anything in Elvish.

Rule No. 517:

A self-respecting man should definitely not know the date on which the Olsen twins become legal.

Rule No. **518**:

The **best** cinematographers are from **Eastern** Europe.

Rule No. **519**:

The best **gaffers** are from the good old U.S. of A.

Rule No. **520**:

If you are a **homeless** man in the movies, you **must** wear **gloves** with the tips of the **fingers** cut off.

Rule No. **521**:

If you are a contestant on a dating reality show, you must keep at least **one** minority around until the second round to prove that you aren't **racist**.

Rule No. **522**:

Sooner or later, all older women start to look like Ann Richards.

Rule No. **523**:

Three **bowling** trophies equals one Ōscar.

Rule No. **524**:

Just because the **bottle** says Bath and Body Works **for Men** doesn't make it right.

Rule No. **525**:

There is no **shame** in a really **good** banana pudding.

Rule No. **526**:

There is only mild shame in a macchiato.

Rule No. **527**:

Movies that feature a fat person in the starring role are invariably sad.

Rule No. **528**:

Or, very, very funny.

Rule No. **529**:

If you **can't** make it good, **make it** big. And if you can't make it big, make it **red**.

Rule No. **531**:

If your PIN number is your **birthday**, you're an idiot.

Rule No. **530**:

If your PIN number is your girlfriend's birthday, you're a sucker.

Rule No. **532**:

The fat kid who **brings** the Jeter **glove** to the ballpark to **catch** a foul—now that's **America.**

Rule No. **533**:

Never be the one to **start**- or finish- a stadium "**wave.**"

Rule No. **534**:

Contrary to popular opinion, the word *can't* should be in your **vocabulary.**

Rule No. **535**:

The **lower** a waiter bends down when **introducing** himself, the less he should **be trusted**.

Rule No. **537**:

The **third** doughnut is always **exactly** one and a half doughnuts **too many**.

Rule No. **536**:

Avoid any restaurant where the daily **specials** are **displayed** by way of plastic **replicas**.

Rule No. 538:

The better looking the person, the more he or she is concerned about the preparation of his or her coffee.

Rule No. 539:

Humor works only on incoming answering-machine messages.

Rule No. 540:

Of all military professions, fighter pilots have the best nicknames. The worst: army cooks.

Rule No. **541**:

The more **talented** the drummer, the less **reliance** on dramatic drumstick **twirling**.

Rule No. **542**:

The more **talented** the lead **guitarist**, the **less** reliance on the **wa-wa pedal**.

Rule No. 543:

The more talented the singer, the less reliance on colorful microphone scarves.

Rule No. 544:

The more talented the lover, the less reliance on colorful condoms.

Rule No. 545:

Nicknaming your penis with a surname preceded by "Senor" will not make you appear more wordly.

Rule No. **546**:

The **angrier** the man, the more **misspellings** in his e-mails.

Rule No. **548**:

A tattoo of a **teardrop** is not a sign of **sensitivity**.

Rule No. **547**:

One **exclamation** point **per** e-mail!

Rule No. **549**:

Especially if it's **on** your penis.

Rule No. **550**:

If the bartender has a **mullet**, ordering a **martini** is probably a **bad** idea.

Rule No. **551**:

Unless you're a **19th-century** president, **lose** the muttonchops.

Rule No. 552:

The more **important** a character in the **bible**, the greater his or her capacity for ferocious **outbursts** of violence **against** underlings.

Rule No. 553:

Disc 2 is the **best** disc in the box set.

Rule No. 554:

The best **villains** have accents and **walk** slowly.

Rule No. 555:

When **wooing** a woman with your **musical** prowess, never opt for an accordion, the **knee cymbals,** or a lute.

Rule No. 556:

Flame **decals** do not fool passerby into **thinking** your car is **"hot."**

Rule No. **557**:

You don't pay cash at the dentist.

Rule No. **558**:

The wackier a doctor's neckties, the less prestigious his medical school.

Rule No. **559**:

If you're in a strip club, and a girl says she's gonna call the manager over, your night just got less fun.

Rule No. **560**:

The **allure** of strip clubs drops **dramatically** when your girlfriend **works** in one.

Rule No. **561**:

No one's ever gotten laid by **wearing** pins with funny **sayings**.

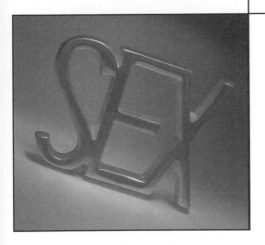

Rule No. **562**:

Leave the **flavored** lip balms to the **preteens** and prostitutes.

Rule No. **563**:

There should **definitely** be a five-day waiting period for **WMD's.**

Rule No. **564**:

The **popcorn** purchased before the movie on the **first date** is always an extra large with butter.

Rule No. **565**:

Anybody who says they "work hard and **play** hard" probably does **neither.**

Rule No. **566**:

People who say they don't **watch** TV mean that they don't fall **asleep** with the TV on.

Rule No. **567**:

The **fatter** the friend, the more he or she will **lecture** you on dietary **advice**.

Rule No. **568**:

Taking a yellow Hi-Liter to a *TV Guide* does not an **academic** make.

Rule No. **569**:

The more **sensitive** the singer-songwriter, the **balder** the crowd.

Rule No. **570**:

A man **wearing** a brightly colored **fanny pack** is precisely seven-eighths of a **man**.

Rule No. **571**:

During the **time** one is standing above the **midget** urinal, one is precisely **two-thirds** of a man.

Rule No. **572**:

Hybrid car equals hybrid man.

Rule No. **573**:

No one ever buys the medium-sized condoms.

Rule No. **574**:

Horizontal stripes on your boxers will not make your penis appear larger.

Rule No. **575**:

There's **no** reason to feel **guilty**: **Firemen** are **annoying** again.

Rule No. **576**:

No matter how **poor** you are, putting your **pennies** in rolls is, economically speaking, a **waste** of time.

Rule No. **577**:

As a group, **brunette** porn stars are more classically **attractive** than **blond** porn stars.

Rule No. 578:

When you die, they will find your porn.

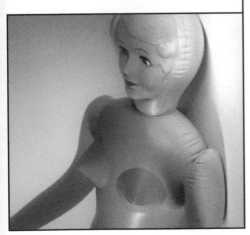

Rule No. 579:

People who whine about smoking are just slightly less annoying than people who whine about a ban on smoking.

Rule No. **580**:

Every **sitcom** must feature an episode in which the **male** character is **tragically** torn celebrating a romantic **milestone** and using unexpected courtside **basketball** tickets.

Rule No. **581**:

A PBS tote bag does not make you an intellectual.

Rule No. **582**:

The secret sauce has no turmeric.

Rule No. **583**:

The quality
of a
take-out
restaurant
is
exactly
mirrored in
the
quality
of its
napkins.

Rule No. **584**:

Soccer would
be a lot more
fun if
everybody used
their hands.

Rule No. **585**:

Denial is good, right up there with bribery.

Rule No. **586**:

Beware the new mommy.

Rule No. **587**:

If you're in the delivery room and your wife's doctor says, "Take a look at this," do not, under any circumstances, take a look.

Rule No. **588**:

Lemme is the best of the faux contractions, followed by *gimme*.

Rule No. **590**:

Your bumper sticker is only 3 percent as clever as you think it is.

Rule No. **589**:

People who laugh at their own jokes are one-tenth as funny as really unfunny people.

Rule No. 591:

The adjective *yummy* should never be used to describe anything beyond food, and then only perhaps once in your adult lifetime.

Rule No. 592:

The adjective *scrumptious* should be used only by the cast of *Chitty Chitty Bang Bang*.

Rule No. **593**:

Beware of restaurants that have **walls** adorned with **anchors**.

Rule No. **594**:

There is no more **extreme** tyrant than the assistant **manager** at your local T.G.I. Friday's.®

Rule No. **595**:

Do not antagonize a man with an **eye patch**.

Rule No. **596**:

A man should **never** own more than two **pairs** of **convertible** pants.

Rule No. **598**:

A man who **pronounces** *croissants* as *"kwa-sa"* is not a **man** at all.

Rule No. **597**:

The funniest **tent** is the yurt, followed by the **tepee** and the wigwam.

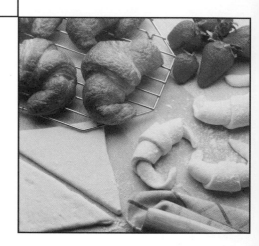

Rule No. **599**:

No bioweapons jokes in the cover letter.

Rule No. **600**:

Mail that comes in envelopes with windows is never good.

Rule No. **601**:

Never trust a woman who refers to her breasts as separate entities (e.g., "the girls").

Rule No. 602:

Popular boys have bad posture, popular girls have good posture.

Rule No. 603:

Toothpicks are not a viable grooming option 50 yards beyond a restaurant.

Rule No. 604:

Flavored dental floss should never be sweeter than the foods that you wish to remove.

Rule No. 605:

Men will travel for sex.

Rule No. 606:

Men will travel for the slimmest, 1 in 1000 Hail Mary possibility of sex.

Rule No. 607:

The longer the limo, the younger the groupies.

index

index

index

index